the day her daisy died

WILLOW PRESTON

this is a story
about blooming
again

thank you
thank you
thank you

there is poetry
in the same creases
as her deodorant
the lipstick smudge
on white teeth
a wobble
while she walks
bony ankles
sweet heart

there is poetry
in the tag sticking out
of her borrowed dress
an unmade bed
flowers picked
to make a messy room
look brighter
a neat life
with little organization

poetry is not just daisies
blooming

it is the dirt
they grow in

she was a warm lick
a lick of fire
a lick of love
she was laughter in a hallway
echoing
an apartment
with wooden floors

occupied by kind people

I fill my life with color and fuzzy blankets and incense that smells like home. I read too many books at once and only finish half. I tell myself I'll get to the others later. my clothes are partly wrinkled and partly ironed. sometimes I forget to hang them up, so they lay in big stacks on my favorite armchair. I look up photos of animals to make myself happy, brewing cups of herbal tea to feel warmth in my stomach. I laugh at silly memories that pop up in my head. then laugh at myself for laughing out loud. I cry when I think of someone dying and promise myself that I will call my sister tomorrow. I have lists of things to do but only occasionally remember to read them. I get distracted by *what ifs* and continue with the *maybes*.

getting lost
and being found
in pretty destinations

she's the incense
you light up
when seeking inspiration

we forgot about the clothes
the lack of clothes
the nakedness
biting at wind
flying kites
with our intestines

hang on

we wandered
through forests
thick with branches
searching for pockets

of light

and we fell into holes
both clear and unclear
where the rope was
to get out

we climbed until
our limbs were stretched
and our bodies
became bloodied

and when we saw the blood

we remembered
how human we were
and we hugged ourselves
until the pain
felt remembered enough

to go away

It is cloudy in Paris
and my balcony
is just high enough
above the city
that I don't have to shout
at people
to watch their steps
or quiet down

I slip my coat on
it fits my shoulders
perfectly

so I do a little wiggle
and grab for an umbrella

maybe I will investigate
how the streets
are
feeling
today

he was an uneven amount of broken
the same way
his cigarette
was an uneven amount of burnt
and hair
an uneven amount of cut
his strides
were a little too quick to keep up with
and sentences
a little too short to understand
people liked him
which he couldn't make sense of
how could so many people
want to be with someone
so lopsided

I put on my sundress
to dance around his big house

I tried on my fancy shoes
clomped around
on white floors

it was all so wide open
so I spun and spun and spun

until he came home
and I hurried
all of my dresses
back into the closet

wiped the scuff marks
from my shoes
he mustn't know I was dancing

because then he will want to dance
with me

and that   is just   for me

she was the kind of girl
that people looked at
because she seemed
familiar

could she be
somebody
that they have seen on TV?

or maybe held
a pleasant conversation with?

was she the girl they saw
on the train yesterday
riding home from work?

or a character
once read in a book
perhaps?

the stares would slip
off her shoulders

she walked with
no recognition
of her beauty

the beauty of causing
people
to feel
like they had met her
before

he can be a poet. he can be a disaster – glass plates shattering, a half-painted wall, a perfume bottle nearly empty, a whiskey bottle mostly full. he can be dry humor – a typewriter with no ribbon, love that crinkles near his eyes, teeth that are nearly perfect. he can be unbrushed hair and a freshly pressed suit. he can smell like sweat or maybe an old book you would find in a library sale. he can be many things all wrapped in skin. mostly, he can be a poet.

where did the honey pots
I hid in my kitchen go

I swear
I thought I put them
next to
the coriander

the thyme has all dried up
the flowers have started to wilt
small spots of sweetness
have become circled with ants

I wash my favorite underwear
in the kitchen sink
the white ones with the roses
please remind me
to get more milk at the store
I need it for my tea
in the morning

sometimes it is nice
 to be elegant
with long finger nails

and sometimes
it is nice to lay
with my puss out to the world

a skirt
that flies upward
and scares everyone

boo!
I'm a woman!

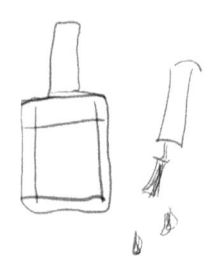

the problem is that I don't know how to let
go of the tired girl. I don't mind the bags I
have set under my eyes. I like to travel and I
like cigarettes. lemon with water fascinates
me. my insides look like coffee grounds,
attracting fruit flies and compost. I wanted
the tired girl. I let her sleep in my front
pocket. scared that if she woke up we might
not know what to do with ourselves. people
might not recognize our glow - or worse-
we might not be cool anymore.

why is it so hard for me
to sit down with my tea
and be in love with you

why must I always want
more sugar

- *when will it be sweet enough*

I wish I could flip
my heart over
like a pillow
on a summer's eve
to feel the cool
on my cheek
again

too many pretty girls
on my mind and
too many men
in my back pocket

the pendulum swings
and sometimes
I don't know
where to stop it

It's not just the daisies
It's the tulips and the stars
It's the lady always dancing
to the music in the yard

It's the cheeks,
the slightest pink
the tongue you touch
with mine
It's the whiskey we ran out of
so we've switched to
homemade wine

It's the guitar that you're learning
just to play one song
It's the lyrics that you're singing
hoping that I'll hum along

grand piano
in her kitchen
white crumbs
on countertops
handpicked roses
from a lover
whose name that she forgets

dresses strewn
across the bedroom
a cat named Kerouac
crazy lady
smart and dainty
a heart you won't get back

he likes his coffee with honey but I like mine black. I need more energy so I sit down and think of ways that I can find some. I used to be a girl scout but now I'm just a girl and the scouts are getting drunk on weekends. weekdays are for working but I don't have a job so I just look at trees and say thank you for providing us air. the caterpillars look nice but my sister said they bite so I decide not to pet them. there's an old treehouse my neighbor built. I climb inside and think about how I'd like another cup of coffee.

I sit in my garden
with my flowers and weeds
and love them all the same

I watched her stride
confidently through the streets
then stop to check herself
in a shop window
as if to make sure
she was
who she thought
she was

- yes, you are still there

the flowers will bloom
where we kept the piano
my bedroom will become
blanketed in green grass
the memories that burnt
will grow
next spring
and we all will
begin again

- *our house burnt in the summertime*

I wore dresses
too heavy for my shoulders
while women cinched my waist
cutting off circulation
to any self confidence

I attended nice dinners
drank out of glasses
too fancy for my fingers
I sipped awkwardly on
conversation and gluttony

cigarette smoke
filled my head
coughing up cries for help

his car was nice
but it drove
the wrong direction
so I rolled out
into the desert
starved of self-love
and found a moment
to hallucinate
in my own discomfort

I stuck out my thumb
and when nobody came
I walked
remembering what it was like
to be alone

neon signs
eventually confirmed
that I am capable
of getting myself
where I want to go

I crept into windows
and watched lovers

fall in love again
with new people
reciting speeches
I had heard before

my eyes drooped
wrists began to feel limp
my glass was full
but my arms were weak
my hair started to dull

the life of the fabulous
was not as rich
as I had expected

nice dinners
left me hungry

It's not the pocket change
weighing you down
It's the *I'll get to it laters*
that seem to grip you
by the ankle

I sit at a bar
alone
and I watch the drinks poor
hand tricks
cherry lips
a laugh from across the room
ice tumbled into a glass
I stare out
in front of me
unsure if I should make conversation
with the bartender
there's an awkward silence
as if we should speak
but neither of us do
until he hands me my drink
and I reply
mercí

- an unspoken understanding that we both are tired

he said that I was cold
but it was his fire
that was not burning
brightly enough

there are spiders in my stomach
and angels in my head
I don't know which to scratch
so, I bite my nails instead

the music is not loud enough
could someone turn it up?
sunbathing in my garden
amongst the buttercups

pour another glass
I'm getting drunk today
not much of a drinker
but it's better than the pain

a princess in her daybed
surrounded by bright gold
heavy with a damp heart
that slowly starts to mold

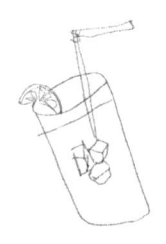

loosen your
grip he said
and the taste
of copper
leaked
from my
tongue
a heaviness
in my heart
became anger
in my head
like a teapot
I rattled

but wait
let me feel
into this
I closed
my eyes
why am I
gripping so
tight
to something
that doesn't
want me
to hold on

I fell
backwards

it
  felt
    good

my addiction
and my eating disorder
are good friends
they walk
hand in hand
to the playground
jumping rope so quickly
that my body
becomes knotted

							- *recess*

*a whole universe
inside of her
but still,
she looks
so lonely*

dear body,

I woke up this morning and wanted to feel you again. for years, I kicked my hunger under the fridge like an ice cube and told her to melt away. but I melted away instead and now my eyes leak when I hear happy songs and bones turn to dust when I'm asked to dance. I told myself I liked the feeling of an empty stomach but the emptier I felt the emptier I became. I lost ten pounds but it was the weight of losing my smile that I noticed the most.

you spent too much time
wallowing in pain
because it felt better
blaming everyone else
for abandoning you
only to realize that
you were starting
to abandon yourself

I turned my back for a second
and before I knew it
four years had gone by
I was twenty-four
looking back on nineteen
because that was the
last time that I
knew myself
really knew myself
and now
I've been spat back
onto the streets
scabs stripped off wounds
I had forgotten to tend
I felt naked
and cold
and nobody could see
that I was shivering
friends were upset
by my lack of care
but what was not
communicated
was my lack of care
for myself
and for the first time
I was alone
in an apartment
thoughtfully decorated
to make me happy

but I was not happy
not yet

memories I had hidden
like grout between tiles
I now needed to scrub
every emotion
became soap suds in my head
pooling out of my eyes
some mornings would be good
others I would cry
the emptiness
of longing to be understood
but I kept going
because despite the pain
there was still a stubborn beating
that I felt deep inside of me
propelling my chest forward
like life had sent
a long-distance mating call
what I once thought was anxiety
had turned to excitement
I began to march along, willingly
and then the march
became a parade
and we all began to dance

I would go back to my apartment
hang my keys on the hook
that I screwed in myself
and sigh
because not only would I feel at
home
but I would feel at home
with myself

I tried to ask
if you could hear me
but the birds
were flapping their wings
and the trees were swaying
and the wind was much too
loud
so you just replied with
what?

I go to the library just to be told that my books are overdue. apparently, I forgot to bring them back last January. I pay the fee while the lady with curly hair looks over her glasses. she wants to ask me why I have a giant coffee stain on my shirt and why I haven't bothered to clean it but knows that would be inappropriate. she presses her lips together to keep from exhaling questionable words while I fumble with my credit card. it is overdue as well but she does not know that. so, I pay my overdue books with my overdue card just to check out new books that will probably be overdue, too.

the city smelt like cocaine
so I dipped my head
inside a low-lit bar
trying to hide from the ants
that were crawling up my legs

the kids all met in Beachwood
and when their teeth began to rot
they started sucking
tits and cocks
to feed their egos
earning bits of money

they used the nickles
not their dimes
to buy themselves new teeth
gnawing at hands
that once fed them

but the city!

rattling, exuberant, perplexing

I wanted to twist my hair
into bows
and hang my clothes
on telephone wires
run naked
through streets
that electrocute me
step into puddles
just to feel a sudden spark

light up my eyes
for one quick second
as I jolt awake
in the dark of my apartment

where I felt for a heartbeat
but all I found
were crumbs in my bed

sometimes

it is hard enough
just to keep moving
but the laundry needs to be
done
and I forgot to call my mother
and did I drink enough water
today?
and I'm starting to forget what it
feels like
to be hugged

the floors are dusty
I feel crumbs under my feet
I keep forgetting to stop at the
mailbox
and I haven't replied to your
messages in days
and please, don't remind me that
my voicemail is full

sometimes,
it is hard enough
just to open my eyes in the
morning
sometimes,
I just want to be honest

but then I just keep going

the truth was starting to hurt   me

the trees peeled back their bark

I howled

I let the daisies
fall out of my hand

I didn't want the flowers
today

the paperboy
delivered news

too loud for my ears
too early in the morning

I am not out of my nightgown yet

he said he loved me
but the goosebumps stung

so I went back
to bed

you make me a cup of tea
to clear my throat
you say I haven't been
talking much
lately

I try to scream but
only air leaves my lungs
i'm running
but my legs don't work

the flowers on the table
need new water
the clothes in my hamper
have not been washed

I cried yesterday
but nobody saw
so my face became hot
my jaw clenched

you touched my back
asked if I could feel anything

but all of the feelings meshed together
and all of my limbs fell to the floor

please, don't pick me up

she swayed
in a velvet skirt
too short for
the unhealed
but
freeing
to the freed

to be sexual
and not intimidated
to be confident
and not judged

there is a woman
who wants to be liberated
while a society
is waiting to
unzip its pants

how do we make sense
of both coexisting
how does she dance
without fear
of being stepped on

please quit stepping on my feet

her life was made up of
constant redirections
turning with no blinker
a sudden jolt
to the side of the road
snapping a quick photo
of a flower
or something

because it's not
ladylike
I yelled the word
cock!
and kicked my heel
into
the air

I hummed
rock music in my head
the rouge on my lips
began to smear

the ladies are wild
they left their dresses
at the the door

now there's only skin
dancing in my apartment
with no recognition
of what we are
or why it matters

yelling into our
open existence
the anger and grace
of being a woman

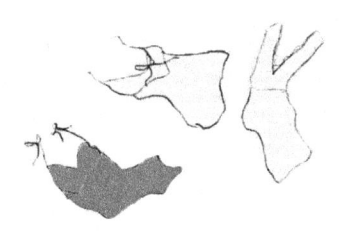

sometimes I feel
my uterus is more
burden
than beauty

sometimes I feel

all they do
is take and take
and leave and leave
and we deal with it

we shove paper napkins
to stop the blood
we wipe the tears
from our children's eyes

others go out
and bang pots with pans
so they won't hear
our screams
while we hum ourselves
hopeful songs

they have made me want to hate
this body I did not choose
these organs I did not create
they have made me want to hate
the magic, the very nature
of being a woman

and I can't stop crying

a man will ask
for a woman who dances
and then get upset
when she dances without him
as if her flow
was going to stop
once the music ended

she will always be a dancer

after the flowers are picked
they die
we place them in water
to watch them suffer
and we think to ourselves
how beautiful

the problem with being a pick-me

my ears keep ringing

I was told
someone from another world
may be trying
to communicate
so I sit and listen

the clothes that I tried on yesterday
are still draped on a chair
I have thoughts of picking them up
that little imaginary figures of myself
dance around

my cat licks his paw
then looks at me
as if to say
quit listening to the ringing
in your ears and move on

but we both keep still
and wait
to see
if anything will happen

and then we all got skinny
but not the kind of skinny
that shows
through wilted skin

the kind of skinny
that bites at our insides
nibbling at our self- worth
saying yes
instead of remembering
that skin is there to set boundaries

each evening
we reapply lipstick
so we can smile
and it won't mean as much
a costume
for a character
we've all decided to play

isn't it exhausting?

to play someone
you don't really
give a fuck about?

maybe that is why
we scorch our insides
with chemicals

because if we cared
about the characters
we were playing
we might actually
take care of them

- *where did we all go?*

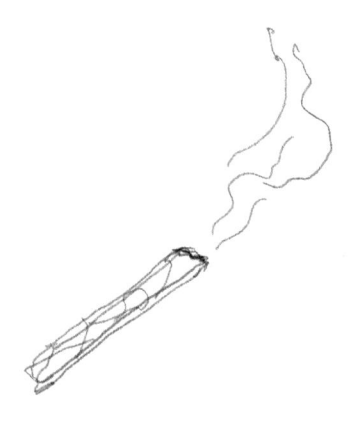

you cried
and I tried to remember
how to catch tears

but my little hummingbird hands
were not quite big enough
to hold them all

so I just flew away

some days
I feel upset by
what you did to me

other days
I scream out
down empty hallways
trying to hear my
pain echo back

I want to
feel something
again

you go on with your life
and collect bodies

while I
dress mine
in clothes
that are too big

so that you will never
feel the need
to touch me
again

*- I hate that you don't know
the trauma you caused*

she warned him not to get too close
I am a wildfire   she said
and wildfires   burn what's beautiful

I am so much more than my body
so, go ahead— chew at my skin
I am mostly bones, anyway

my soul will remain

and you will have something
stuck in your teeth

> *— he said that he would eat me alive*

I am sorry for watching you
wilt in my hands

I should have given you
more water

- the day her daisy died

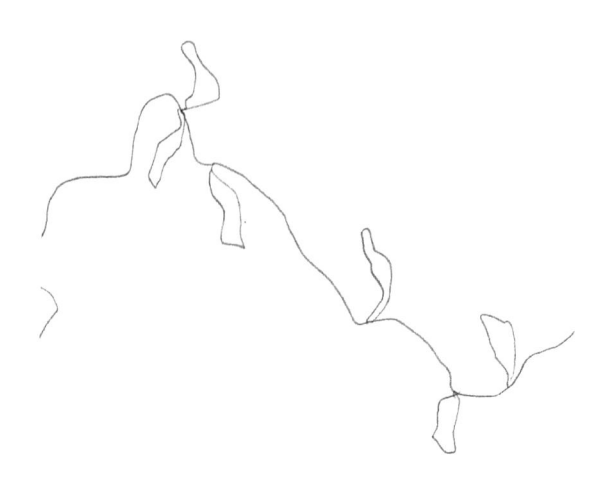

blooming

I couldn't sleep

maybe it was the toxins leaving my body
maybe it was the help
I was frantically seeking
fizzing up in my head

maybe it was my body repairing itself
from the years of damage
I had done

maybe
I was finally waking up
and that is why
I felt so restless

my body excited
for its new beginning

not getting my fix
gave me headaches

maybe
It was not from
the lack of substance

maybe
It was the pain that I was trying to
hide from
returning to me

and instead of being scared this time
I said *hello pain, I am happy to feel you again*

and maybe, one day, eventually

my pain will not be afraid to show itself
and I will not be afraid to feel it

my plants look mostly alive
because I keep trimming off the dead parts

if I were to stop trimming
my plants would look mostly dead

what made her beautiful
was that she was not afraid of life
life was more afraid of her

ripping through sails
biting glassware
a tiger would *rawr*
and she would *purr* back
making it jump
with her gentle vibrations

she made it look easy
to be so free
and made sure that
everyone

would get a chance
to share a dance
with freedom

scream
yelled the trees
and the birds flew

cry
ran the river
and the fish jumped

move
felt the mountains
and the snow fell

breathe
said the sky
and her lungs filled

I started checking
in all my favorite
hiding places
confused as to
how I could lose myself

only to realize
that I wasn't lost

I just had been busy
looking for shadows
instead of
my light

- I had been shining the whole time

my body felt free today
I floated on water
nourished myself
with vegetables and sunshine
shared space
with close friends
I smiled
a real smile
and felt a feeling
both unfamiliar
and correct
the feeling
of freedom
of floating
of releasing
calmness flowed over me
and it landed
at my heart

thank you

I felt her

I allowed her to sweep over my body
filling the pieces
of chipped away bone
relieving thousands of years
worth of water

the pain of my ancestors
my mother
myself
crying until
every being in my family chain
was acknowledged

I felt you
I can feel you
the water spilling upon my cheeks
evaporated

my loved ones patted my shoulders
saying *thank you*
for taking the time
because
feeling
is the first step
in healing

and onward we go

- taking the time to feel

I did not want
to just soak in my light
I wanted to dance with her
like two children
playing a game of tag
and laughing

- having fun with my light

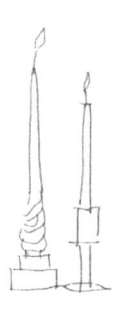

it is the sky
who shouts for us
howling
into our feminine

it is the freedom
dancing with
our tenderness
nurturing
our bodies

it is the wind
that blows through strong hair
energizing our want
to not be so damn perfect
all the time
reminding us
of our nature

it is the love
that stings our fingers
and stains your heart

it is wanting to be accepted
for what we are
and not for some
idea of yours

I drink honey
with my tea
place rose petals
on my eyelids

the afternoon will come
we will clink glasses
and reminisce
on how our mornings
have been

the pain
of breaking though
thick skin
generations
worth of soil
chasing the
sunlight
she was
curly hair
created by a
universe of emotions
that she wanted
to release
p
u

into the sky

- *growing pains*

she was tired
of staring at herself
in the mirror
she wanted a poem
something tangible

she wanted to understand
the softness
in her eyes
and why
her heart
was always
on fire

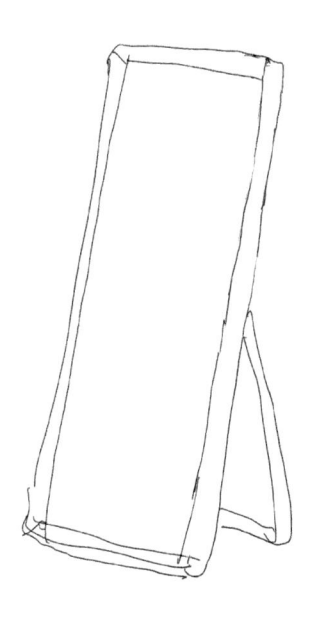

I started thinking more
or maybe it was less
about what life should be
and suddenly I remembered
not to think at all
but to sink deeper
into the love
I had for it
already

I see you
the way you look at shiny things
I watch you look at trees
like you look at mountains
like you look at me

I thank you for that look
of curiosity
of hope
of love

because that look
is what life
is all about
and you bring it
everywhere you go

- thank you for looking at me like that

I am more divine
than the apple you eat
the wine
you ordered for dinner

I am much more divine
than the skin
that shines in the light
the toes
you suck on
the silk
that slides down my legs

my divinity is more than
your words
your touch
your money

my divinity is not defined by
what you get from me
or what I get from you

my divinity
is what attracted you to me
to begin with

my divinity
is a golden root
that grows throughout my body
every day, getting thicker
and you are a mealybug

sucking at my sap
I will not allow it
any longer

she did not wait
for the world
to open up for her
she opened it herself
with small, magical fingers
she searched for the cracks
to pry it all open

- she wasn't a waiter

today
I do not feel like
keeping up with
the buzzing

instead
I will pour myself
a cup of tea
and let the silence
love me

it is okay to protect your identity
you do not always have to share yourself
you do not owe anyone, anything

- *boundaries*

she called them moon sparkles
she was my moon sparkle

there is a sign
that blinks in neon
that I am slowly starting
to look away from

I drive my dusty car
down dusty streets

lotto tickets
aren't as mesmerizing
when you have a dream
to work towards

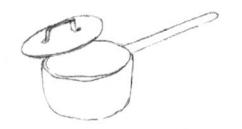

I let go

of the masculine urge
to grip
and only then
began my flow

of promise
of entanglement
of leaps of faith
and gentle landings

dancing
with my feminine

- *she will take you many places*

she was folk music
and windy hair

she was dancing
with no idea
people were watching

she was a curtsy
I was a bow
everyone clapping
at her light show

some days
magic tastes like
bitter coffee
others
like cinnamon

in some ways
it is silent
in others
it is the music
that pulses
deep within

there are girls
who brush their hair
every other day

who show up to the party happy
and walk to the coffee shop exhausted

there are girls with apartments
in small frames
stairs that lead up to rooftops
they can't see the stars from
the city lights are too bright

they gravitate towards
brick buildings
multicolored flowering pots
they talk shit
as much as they write poetry
and love
as much as they want it

they think they want it
but will sometimes hide instead of
feeling things

they throw their clothes
onto another chair
and take a bath
because sometimes it is warmer
to take a bath
than try to find love
in strange people

there are girls with quick wits
and bad jokes who often wish to go lie
in a field somewhere
thinking no one will look for them

although people will look for them
because they are the sparks
even though they try to dull themselves
with cigarette smoke
and stomach aches

they are irreplaceable
undeniably, exuberantly, exquisite

there are girls who need to be reminded
of the bounce in their step
the honesty in their eyes
the desire to feel well
and do better

there are people cheering them on
they are the dancers
they are the artists
the leaders
the oh so magnificent
and we are all in this
together

so with the next flower pot you see
have a little laugh with yourself
and think of all of the girls
who thought
how pretty

find the people you can scream with
without them asking why you're screaming

an unspoken understanding
of just
letting it all out

your pain is felt
let our voices
come together
and feel
like a hug

- *you are heard*

the sunflowers
were on their tippy toes

reeeeeeaaching to say

hello

to you

oh let me be
your bumblebee
and spread some sweet
to you

flowers
in her honeypot
a tincture
for his brew

dancing on white tables
no roof above our heads
buzzing! skies the limit!
we keep our spirits fed

to love the stillness
as much as you
love the rush

to not know which you desire more

- she fits perfectly into them both

this year I learnt the act of caring. the small enjoyment of doing the dishes, taking notice of the items I bring into my home, making my bed, nourishing my body. this year I began to understand why my mother would hum as she'd sweep the floors and the simple pleasure of homemade soup, fresh groceries, soft clothing. I began to love my body for the way it took me places and not just the way it looked. everyday I became more impressed with my decisions, trusting myself, caring about the people I met with each interaction. I learnt the act of caring, genuinely taking notice of the small pleasures around me, the small tasks, the bright smiles. the simple act of caring. It feels good.

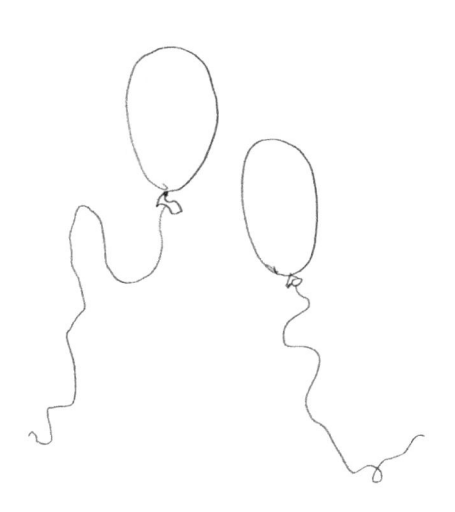

I think I am tired
because I have given so much of
myself
to everyone else

my body is starting
to ache

it no longer wants to be felt
only freed

longing for those
who will watch
and not grasp

for something
to hold on to

I wasn't meant
to lay in a bed
and let vines
grow over me

I am
a bloomer
a dance in the sun
kind of lady

I smile with teeth
and cry into the wind
praying that it all
will never end

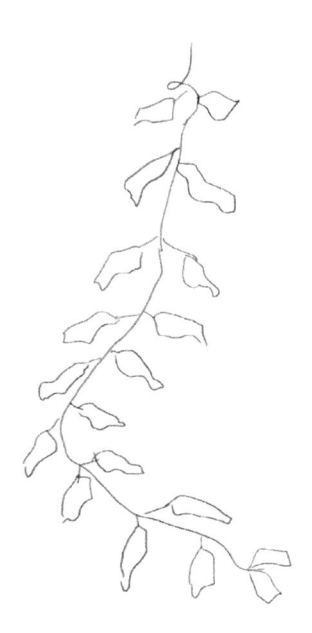

he had written me in
as a character
for his fantasy

and then became bitter
when he realized
that I was too big
for the part

- I will never be small

she was not scared
of the aloneness
she bathed herself
in quiet chatter
within her own mind
and when she was ready
allowed the right people
to soak in it
with her

I started to love
the way the sheets fit around
my body
not shuddering
when I felt my thighs touch
how my ankles look in socks
skirts that show my legs
hair pushed behind my ear
a face that smiles
in the sunlight

you see
I take notice of these things
as if they are marks on a wall
I had made to measure
myself
my whole identity
dependant on a size
that has always caused me to
suck in

for the first time
I relaxed my body
and didn't judge what I saw

I exhaled

I have learned
to say

thank you

the child I had hidden
started to uncurl her body

you are safe now
I whispered

you are safe, here

thank you   she replied

thank you

from patterned braids
she let her hair loose
dancing through mud
licking sweat
howling *yes!*
as the wind carries her voice
to the next spot of landing
soft grass
wild roots
animals
inhaling her exhale

she is
a woman of the day
and the night
kisses
with the morning

- an ode to the fearless woman

she never let go of love
and that is why
her heart
still blooms
a garden

gratitude

to the loves in my life
to the mirrors
the dancers
the magicians

thank you for your support

to Maddy McKeever for her sweet illustrations
to Jon Davis for his skillful revisions

thank you for creating with me

thank you to *you*

for picking this book up
and for picking yourslef
every day

>   *I love you*
>   *I love you*
>   *I love you*

if you feel the call
to follow for more

@thedayherdaisydied
@willowwpreston

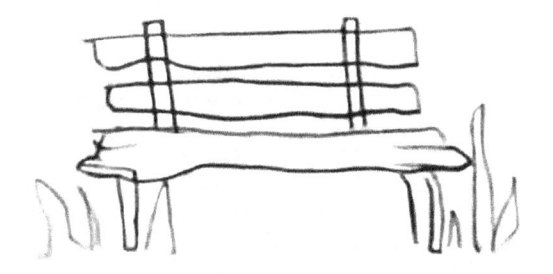

Copyright © 2023 by Willow Preston

All rights reserved.

No portion of this book may be reproduced in any form without written permission from the publisher or author, except as permitted by U.S. copyright law.

@willowwpreston @thedayherdaisydied

Printed in the USA
CPSIA information can be obtained
at www.ICGtesting.com
LVHW010437250923
759090LV00065B/1083